FRANCHISING IN NEPAL 2014

Legal and Business Considerations

KENDAL H. TYRE, JR., EXECUTIVE EDITOR
DIANA VILMENAY-HAMMOND, MANAGING EDITOR
PIERCE HAESUNG HAN, ASSISTANT EDITOR

LEXNOIR FOUNDATION

SECOND QUARTER 2014

LexNoir Foundation is the charitable, educational arm of LexNoir, an international network of lawyers connecting the African Diaspora.

This publication, *Franchising in Nepal 2014: Legal and Business Considerations*, contains excerpts from *Franchising in Asia 2014: Legal and Business Considerations*. Both works are published by LexNoir Foundation and reflect the points of view of the authors and editors as of the date of publication and do not necessarily represent the opinions, interpretations, or positions of the law firms or organizations with which they are affiliated, nor the opinions, interpretations or positions of LexNoir Foundation or LexNoir.

Nothing contained in this book is to be considered as the rendering of legal advice, either generally or in connection with any specific issues or case. Readers are responsible for obtaining advice from their own legal counsel or other professional. This book, any forms and agreements or other information herein are intended for educational and informational purposes only.

www.lexnoir.org

Table of Contents

Page

Bibliography of International Franchise Resources

Kendal H. Tyre, Jr., Diana Vilmenay-Hammond, Pierce Haesung Han, Courtney L. Lindsay II and Keri McWilliams
Nixon Peabody LLP

Acknowledgment

This book could not have been written without the hard work and dedication of each of the contributing authors and editors. Thank you.

We would like to acknowledge and extend our heartfelt gratitude to Maria Stallings of the Washington, D.C. office of Nixon Peabody LLP for her invaluable assistance in revising, proofing, and editing this publication.

About the Editors and Authors

Kendal H. Tyre, Jr. – Kendal is a partner in the Washington, D.C. office of Nixon Peabody LLP. He handles domestic and cross-border transactions, including mergers and acquisitions, joint ventures, strategic alliances, licensing, and franchise matters.

In his franchise and licensing practice, Kendal counsels domestic and international franchisors, franchisees, licensors, licensees and distributors regarding U.S. state and federal franchise laws as well as foreign franchise legislation in a variety of jurisdictions. Kendal drafts and provides advice with regard to franchise and license agreements, disclosure documents and area development agreements and has extensive experience drafting and negotiating a variety of other commercial agreements. His client base spans the United States and foreign countries, including South Africa, Kenya, and the United Kingdom.

Kendal is a frequent contributor to franchise publications and a frequent speaker at franchise programs held by the American Bar Association Forum on Franchising and the International Franchise Association.

Kendal is co-chair of the firm's Diversity Action Committee and its Africa Group. Kendal is also the executive director of LexNoir Foundation.

E-mail address: ktyre@nixonpeabody.com

Diana Vilmenay-Hammond – Diana is an attorney in the Washington, D.C. office of Nixon Peabody LLP. She is a member of the firm's Franchise & Distribution team.

In her franchise practice, Diana works with domestic and international franchisors on transactional and litigation matters. Specifically, she counsels franchisor clients regarding state and federal franchise laws, disclosure and registration obligations. Diana drafts and negotiates various commercial agreements, including international franchise and development agreements.

Diana has co-authored numerous articles on franchising and frequently co-hosted the Nixon Peabody franchise law webinar series. Topics have included:

- "Franchise Case Law Round-Up: Implications for Your Franchise;"
- "Social Media Part II: Best Practices in Protecting Your Brand in the New Media;" and
- "The Awuah Case: Bellwether or Outlier."

Diana received her J.D. from Howard University School of Law and her B.A. from Georgetown University. She is a member of the American Bar Association (Forum on Franchising).

E-mail address: dvilmenay@nixonpeabody.com

Pierce Haesung Han – Pierce is an associate in Nixon Peabody's Global Business & Transactions group. Pierce focuses his practice on three main areas, assisting clients with a variety of complex business transactions.

- Mergers & Acquisitions: Providing assistance to both public and private clients with various mergers and acquisitions, performing due diligence, drafting and negotiating transaction documents, and facilitating closing and post-closing mechanics.
- International Commercial Transactions: Drafting and negotiating a variety of commercial agreements, including international franchise and development agreements, license agreements, and purchase and sale agreements.

- Federal Securities Law Matters: Assisting public and private clients regarding federal securities laws and stock exchange rules relating to corporate governance and disclosure.

Pierce serves as the Secretary of the Asian Pacific Bar Association Educational Fund (an affiliate of the Asian Pacific American Bar Association of the Greater Washington, D.C. Area).

Pierce received his J.D. from Georgetown University Law Center and his B.A. from Case Western Reserve University. He is admitted to practice in the State of New York and the District of Columbia.

E-mail address: phan@nixonpeabody.com

Courtney L. Lindsay II – Courtney is an associate in Nixon Peabody's Corporate and Finance practice. In his corporate practice, Courtney assists for-profit and non-profit entities with transactional matters and corporate governance. In various capacities, Courtney has been involved in multiple merger and acquisition transactions, including drafting and managing due diligence.

Previously, Courtney worked in the legal and business affairs department at a national cable network, where he handled matters related to the network's LLC agreement, including drafting board and member consent agreements.

Courtney received his J.D. from the University of Virginia School of Law and his B.A. from the University of Virginia. He is admitted to practice in the Commonwealth of Virginia and the District of Columbia.

E-mail address: clindsay@nixonpeabody.com

Keri McWilliams – Keri is an associate in the Franchise & Distribution team of Nixon Peabody LLP. Keri works with clients on a number of franchising issues, including obtaining and maintaining franchise registrations in various states, responding to state inquiries regarding trade practices, ongoing compliance with state and federal regulations, and updating franchise disclosure documents. She also handles franchise sales counseling and franchise system issues.

Keri is a member of the American Bar Association's Forum on Franchising, and the Federal and Minnesota State bar associations. She is also a member of Minnesota Women Lawyers and the Minnesota Association of Black Lawyers, and a volunteer in the Volunteer Lawyers Network.

Keri received her J.D. from the Georgetown University Law Center and her B.F.A. from Washington University. She is admitted to practice in the District of Columbia and Minnesota.

E-mail address: kmcwilliams@nixonpeabody.com

Devendra Pradhan – Devendra is the Founder and Managing Member of Pradhan & Associates. Before establishing Pradhan & Associates, Devendra worked with various law firms in Kathmandu for several years. He also worked with various law firms in New York and Washington, D.C. In addition to Nepal, Devendra is also admitted as an attorney at law in New York, the District of Columbia and various federal courts in the United States. Devendra focuses his practice on advising and representing foreign companies primarily in the area of aviation, telecommunications, technology, banking and finance, mergers & acquisitions, private equity, intellectual property, commercial arbitration, cross-border and international transactions, etc. He has been recognized as a leading lawyer in various areas of commercial law by *Who's Who Legal*, *Chambers Global* and *Chambers Asia*. *Who's Who Legal* has recognized him amongst the world's leading lawyers in the area of aviation, M&A, project finance and trademark for the last several years. Devendra regularly contributes scholarly articles on various topics of Nepalese commercial laws and on key issues of international laws in various national publications as well as in international law journals and international publications. Devendra received his bachelor's degree in law at Tribhuvan University in Kathmandu, Nepal in 1990. He later received his LL.M. in International Business Law in 2001 from American University, Washington College of Law in Washington, D.C.

E-mail address: dpradhan@pradhanlaw.com

Shirshak Ghimire – Shirshak is an associate at Pradhan & Associates. Shirshak works in the areas of aviation, banking and finance, trade and commerce, corporate finance, M&A, technology, projects, telecommunication, etc. Shirshak received his B.A. and LL.B. from the National Law School of India University in Bangalore, India in 2011.

E-mail address: sghimire@pradhanlaw.com

About the Book

Franchising in Nepal 2014: Legal and Business Considerations contains excerpts from the larger work *Franchising in Asia 2014: Legal and Business Considerations.* Both books serve as practical, succinct, easy-to-use reference tools for lawyers, business people and academics to use in navigating the laws and business issues impacting franchise arrangements in Asia.

This book provides an overview of the franchise industry in Nepal and addresses the typical legal issues confronted when expanding a franchise system in Nepal. The larger work, *Franchising in Asia 2014: Legal and Business Considerations*, covers those laws governing franchising in several other Asian countries.

In both books, an author, who is a legal expert in the designated jurisdiction, addresses the basic questions that a franchise lawyer would need to know to competently represent a client in expanding their franchise system to that country.

Each country chapter organizes a discussion of that country's laws under various headings and in a uniform format. Topics were sent to each country's author in the form of a questionnaire, and each author drafted responses to the questions presented. A general overview relating to the political and economic history of the country at the beginning of each chapter provides an initial context for the regulatory framework.[1]

---

1 The source of information for these sections is the Central Intelligence Agency, https://www.cia.gov/library/publications/the-world-factbook/ (last visited June 2, 2014).

Apart from an overview of the legal framework for franchising, each book contains other articles and resources that should prove useful to those in the franchise industry.

The authors for each chapter are listed at the beginning of a chapter and their biographical information is listed in the previous section, *About the Editors and Authors*.

Readers should always consult with local counsel in the relevant jurisdiction instead of relying solely on the information contained in this book. The laws governing franchising are evolving and local counsel in Nepal are best positioned to provide timely, relevant advice applying the current law to the particular facts of a case.

Franchising in Nepal

Devendra Pradhan and Shirshak Ghimire
Pradhan & Associates
Kathmandu, Nepal

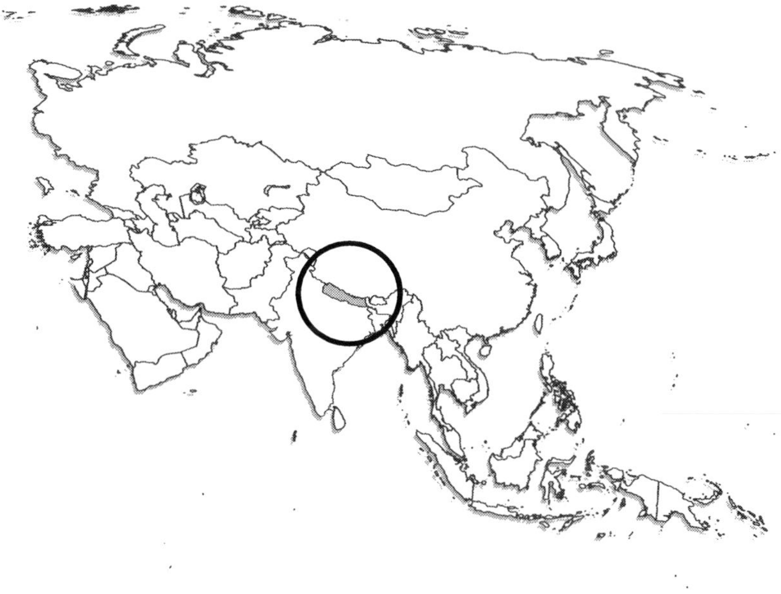

Nepal

I. Introduction

A. Historical Background of the Country

In 1951, the Nepali monarch ended the century-old system of rule by hereditary premiers and instituted a cabinet system of government. Reforms in 1990 established a multiparty democracy within the framework of a constitutional monarchy. An insurgency led by Maoists broke out in 1996. The ensuing 10-year civil war between Maoist and government forces witnessed the dissolution of the cabinet and parliament and assumption of absolute power by the king in 2002.

Several weeks of mass protests in April 2006 were followed by several months of peace negotiations between the Maoists and government officials, and culminated in a late 2006 peace accord and the promulgation of an interim constitution. Following a nationwide election in April 2008, the newly formed Constituent Assembly ("Assembly") declared Nepal a federal democratic republic and abolished the monarchy at its first meeting the following month. The Assembly elected the country's first president in July. Between 2008 and 2011 there were four different coalition governments, led twice by the United Communist Party of Nepal-Maoist, which received a plurality of votes in the 2008 Assembly election, and twice by the Communist Party of Nepal-United Marxist-Leninist ("UML").

After the Assembly failed to draft a constitution by the May 2012 deadline set by the Supreme Court, then Prime Minister Baburam Bhattarai dissolved the Assembly. Months of negotiations ensued until March 2013 when the major political parties agreed to create an interim government headed by then Chief Justice Khil Raj Regmi with a mandate to hold elections for a new Assembly.

Elections were held in November 2013, in which the Nepali Congress won the largest share of the seats in the Assembly. In February 2014, a coalition government with the second place UML was formed and with Nepali Congress President Sushil Koirala as prime minister.

B. Economy of the Country

Nepal is heavily dependent on remittances, which amounts to as much as 22-25% of GDP. Agriculture is the mainstay of the economy, providing a livelihood for more than 70% of the population and accounting for a little over one-third of GDP. Industrial activity mainly involves the processing of agricultural products, including pulses, jute, sugarcane, tobacco, and grain. Nepal has considerable scope for exploiting its potential in hydropower, with an estimated 42,000 MW of commercially feasible capacity. Additional challenges to Nepal's growth include its landlocked geographic location, persistent power shortages, underdeveloped transportation infrastructure, civil strife and labor unrest, and its susceptibility to natural disaster. The lack of political consensus in the past several years has delayed national budgets and prevented much-needed economic reform, although the government passed a full budget in 2013.

C. Franchise Legal Overview

Though Nepal does not have franchise specific legislation, a number of laws, regulations, procedures and directives are applicable in franchise agreements, notably– (i) *Agency Act 1957*, (ii) *Agency Rules 1963*, (iii) *Contract Act 2000*, (iv*) Foreign Investment and Technology Transfer Act 1992*, (v) *Income Tax Act 2002*, (vi) *Value Added Tax Act 1996*, (vii) *Customs Act 2007*, (viii) *Foreign Exchange Regulation Act 1962*, (ix) *Arbitration Act 1999*, (x) *Patent*

Design Trademark Act 1965 and (xi) the *Procedural Manual for Foreign Investment in Nepal 2012.*

II. Regulatory Requirements

A. Pre-Sale Disclosure

Please describe any pre-sale franchise disclosure or similar requirements that may apply to franchise transactions.

There are no pre-sale franchise disclosure requirements applicable to the franchise agreements in Nepal.

B. Governmental Approvals, Registrations, Filing Requirements

Please describe any necessary government approvals, registrations, or filing requirements that may apply to franchise transactions.

In the context of Nepal, franchising can be seen as the equivalent of a "technology transfer" under the *Foreign Investment and Technology Transfer Act 1992* ("FITTA"), which is the primary law governing technology transfer in Nepal. A technology transfer under the FITTA constitutes an agreement between a local industry and a foreign investor on the following matters:

- use of any technological right, specialization, formula, process, patent or technical know-how of foreign origin;
- use of any trademark of foreign ownership; or
- acquiring any foreign technical, consultancy, management and marketing service[2].

---

2 *FITTA*, §2(c).

Licensing of the intellectual property rights, its business model and know-how by a foreign entity to a local entity will fall under the definition of "technology transfer" under the FITTA. Any kind of technology transfer from a foreign entity to a local entity requires the approval of the Department of Industry ("DOI")[3]. In case the patent, design or trademark is already registered in Nepal, the owner of such intellectual property may assign the rights to or license the usage of such intellectual property under the *Patent Design Trademark Act 1965* ("PDTA") with approval from DOI[4]. For obtaining such approval, the DOI must be provided with:

- Technology Transfer Agreement, Licensing Agreement or the Deed of Assignment;
- Corporate Documents of the Franchisor, Licensor or Assignor; and
- Industry Registration Certificate of the Franchisee, Licensee or Assignee.

Generally, the approval is granted within a month after the application for approval is made[5].

Franchising may cover the use of technological rights, intellectual property rights or distribution of products. In the event a local entity is involved solely in the distribution of a foreign entity's products, then the provision of the *Agency Act 1957* ("Agency Act") shall be applicable. The definition of an agent includes a distributor or representative.[6] Where an agency agreement has been entered into, the agent is required to be registered with the Department of Commerce after submitting necessary information about the nature of the agency including the agreement between the two entities, the price list, tax registration certificate and the applicable incorporation documents, along with certain registration fees as collateral.[7]

---

3 *Id.*, §3(1).

4 *PDTA*, §21D.

5 *FITTA*, §3(3).

6 *Agency Act*, §2(a).

7 *Id.*, §4.

C. Limits on Fees and Typical Term of Franchise Agreement

Please describe any limits upon the nature and extent of fees and the term of a typical franchise agreement.

No limit has been prescribed on the nature and rate of the franchise fees and the term of a typical franchise agreement. The approval of the terms and conditions of the franchise agreement by the DOI will depend upon the nature of the technology and other technical expertise being transferred.

III. Currency

If all payments under a franchise agreement must be made in immediately available U.S. Dollars, please advise as to any restrictions, reporting requirements, or regulations concerning the exchange, repatriation or remittance of U.S. Dollars.

The franchisee can apply to the DOI for the repatriation of franchise fees as per the agreement. To do so, the franchisee has to submit the calculation of the amount due to the franchisor certified by the auditor along with the certificate of payment of income tax on royalty as per the prevailing tax rate.[8]

According to the *Foreign Exchange Regulation Act 1962* ("FERA"), any kind of foreign currency transaction including payment of royalty in foreign exchange requires the approval of the Central Bank, i.e. the *Nepal Rastra Bank* ("NRB").[9] Foreign currency transaction includes any payment made in foreign exchange.[10] A franchisor is

---

8 *Procedural Manual for Foreign Investment in Nepal 2012* ("PMFIN"), Para 3.2.4.

9 *Id*, §3.

allowed to repatriate the franchise fees due under the technology transfer agreement.[11]

IV. Taxes, Tariffs, and Duties

Please do not provide any in-depth comments on tax structuring. However, please provide your general comments on the typical amount of withholding tax that would apply and whether a "gross-up" provision contained in a franchise agreement would be enforceable in your country.

The *Income Tax Act 2002* ("ITA") defines "royalty" as the payment for the conferment of rights in any intangible property including usage or licensing of intellectual property rights, technology transfer and other know-how.[12] A withholding tax of 15% is levied upon any payment of royalty on an intangible property for which Nepal is its source.[13] The ITA also allows for a 50% tax concession on income derived from a service charge or a royalty for a technology transfer provided by a franchisor for the industries established in any special economic zone.[14] The ITA also provides a 25% exemption on the income tax levied on the royalty earned from the import of intellectual property and a 50% concession on income tax levied upon the income earned from the transfer of assignment of intellectual property in a franchise agreement.[15]

The *Value Added Tax Act 1996* ("VAT Act") imposes Value Added Tax ("VAT") over goods and services supplied, imported to, or exported from Nepal.[16] The VAT

---

10 *FERA*, §2(d1).
11 *Id.*, §10C(5).
12 *ITA*, §2(aa).
13 *Id.*, §88(1).
14 *Id.*, §11 (3A) (d) as added by Finance Act of 2013-14.
15 *Id.*, §§11(3I), 11(3J) as added by Finance Act of 2013-14.
16 *VAT Act*, §5(1).

Act defines goods as any moveable or immoveable property,[17] and services as anything other than goods.[18] The services provided by a foreign entity to a Nepalese entity including conferment of rights pertaining to copyright, patent, license, trademark and other such intellectual property rights are considered as providing service under the purview of the VAT Act.[19] The VAT Act imposes VAT at the rate of 13% on all goods and services including franchise services.[20]Any goods exported from Nepal and any service provided to a person not having a business or legal presence in Nepal is charged VAT at the rate of zero per cent.[21]

According to the Customs Act, the customs value of goods to be imported are determined on the basis of the transaction value of such goods based on the rules on customs valuation, annexes and explanatory notes set forth in the *Agreement on Implementation of Article VII of the General Agreement on Tariffs and Trade 1994.*[22] Therefore, the payments regarding patents, trademarks and copyrights are added to the price actually paid or payable for the imported goods in determining their customs value.

Nepal has signed double taxation agreements with India, Qatar, China, Austria, Republic of Korea, Mauritius, Norway, Pakistan, Sri Lanka and Thailand.

No restrictions have been placed upon "gross up" clauses which shall be guided by the franchise agreement.

---

17 *Id.*, §2(e).
18 *Id.*, §2(f).
19 *Id.*, §8(2) as added by Finance Act of 2013-14.
20 *Id.*, §7(1) as added by Finance Act of 2013-14.
21 *Id.*, Schedule 2.
22 *Customs Act*, §13(1).

V. Trademarks

Please advise us as to whether there are any special requirements for granting a valid trademark license, including the use of a registered user agreement or a short trademark license agreement and any required filing of such an agreement with the trademark authorities.

Trademarks registered in Nepal can be licensed or assigned through a joint application by both the franchisor and the franchisee to the DOI.[23] The rights of the franchise shall be as stated in the agreement. However, the statutory rights granted to the owner of a trademark can only apply when the trademark is registered within Nepal.[24] DOI will register the license/assignment only after all the requisite procedures have been met.

VI. Restrictions on Transfer

Please advise as to whether there are any restrictions (1) on a franchisor to restrict transfers by a master franchisee, any interest in a master franchisee, or the assets of the master franchisee or (2) the ability of a master franchisee to control and/or restrict transfers of a subfranchisee's rights under a master franchise agreement, an interest in the subfranchisee, or the assets of the subfranchisee.

There are no restrictions on a franchisor to restrict (i) transfers by a master franchisee, (ii) any interest in a master franchisee, (iii) the assets of the master franchisee, (iv) the ability of a master franchisee to control and/or restrict transfers of a subfranchisee's rights under a master franchise agreement, (v) interest in the subfranchisee, or (vi) the assets of the subfranchisee.

---

23 *PDTA*, §21D.

24 *Id.*, §21B.

VII. Termination

Please advise us as to any laws relating to termination in your country, such as agency laws, required indemnity provisions, notice or "good cause" requirements, or other laws affecting termination of a franchise agreement. Please describe.

There are no specific laws regulating termination of franchise agreements in Nepal. The general law of contract under the *Contract Act 2000* ("Contract Act") shall apply to franchise agreements. The parties to a contract are granted freedom to choose the terms and conditions of the contract, including the termination provisions.[25]

In the event the violation of the terms of the franchise agreement also results in the violation of the terms of the registered agency under the Agency Act, the agent may be subject to a fine and a five year ban from engaging in agency business.[26]Agency may be transferred through an application with a deed of consent from the registered agent and that of the principal company.[27]

VIII. Governing Law, Jurisdiction, and Dispute Resolution

A. Choice of Law of Foreign Jurisdiction

Please confirm whether the choice of law of a foreign jurisdiction would likely to be upheld under the law of the country, except for certain matters such as trademarks, bankruptcy and competition matters, which we assume would be governed by the law in your country.

---

25 *Contract Act*, §5.
26 *Agency Act*, §7.
27 *Agency Rules*, Rule 7.

In any dispute arising between a franchisor and franchisee, the parties are required, first, to attempt to resolve their rights amicably, in the presence of the DOI. If that fails, the parties shall settle such dispute through arbitration under the prevailing arbitration rules of the United Nations Commission on International Trade Law ("UNCITRAL"). In such case, Kathmandu must be the venue of arbitration and the arbitration proceedings are subject to the laws of Nepal.[28] For industries with fixed assets above NPR500 million (approximately US$5,261,500), disputes may be settled as mentioned in the franchise agreement where the parties may select the choice of law and jurisdiction of their choice.[29] Therefore, industries with investments up to NPR500 million (approximately US$5,261,500) or less must choose Nepalese law as the choice of law.

B. International Arbitration Dispute Resolution

Please confirm that a court in your country would honor an election of international arbitration dispute resolution, and therefore refuse to hear any disputes arising under a franchise agreement.

Nepalese courts will honor selection of international arbitration as the method of resolving dispute provided the parties have attempted to amicably resolve the disputes in the presence of the DOI. Nepal is a signatory to the *Convention on the Recognition and Enforcement of Foreign Arbitral Awards* (the "New York Convention"). According to the *Arbitration Act 1999* ("Arbitration Act") foreign arbitral awards are enforceable in Nepal on reciprocal basis, if the following conditions are met:

---

28 *FITTA*, §7

29 *PMFIN*, Pg. 63

- the arbitrator has been appointed and the award has been made according to the laws and procedure mentioned in the agreement;
- the parties had been notified about the arbitration proceedings in time;
- the decision is according to the conditions mentioned in the agreement or confined only to the subject matters referred to the arbitrator;
- the decision has become final and binding on the parties according to the laws of the country where the decision was decided;
- the laws of the country of the petitioner or the laws of the country where arbitration proceedings have been conducted do not contain any provisions stating that arbitration award taken in Nepal cannot be implemented; and
- the application has been filed for the implementation of the award within 90 days from the date of award.[30]

However, a foreign arbitral award will not be enforced (i) when the dispute is of such a nature which could not have been resolved through arbitration under Nepalese laws, or (ii) when the enforcement of the foreign arbitral award would be contrary to the public policy of Nepal.

IX. Non-Competition Provisions

If the franchise agreement prohibits the franchisee from engaging in certain competitive activities during the term of the agreement, and for a 12-month period after the termination or expiration of the agreement, please comment on the enforceability of non-competition covenants in your country.

30 *Arbitration Act*, §34(2).

Pertaining to any contractual provisions under franchise agreements, the following would not be considered as being restrictive of trade:

- a clause preventing the seller of the business and goodwill associated with it from engaging in a similar business or trade at a specified time and place; or
- a clause preventing any individual from receiving the service of any other entity for a specified period of time after the termination of services from the particular entity.[31]

Therefore, a provision of the agreement prohibiting the master franchisee from engaging in certain competitive activities during the term of the agreement, or for a 12-month period after the termination or expiration of the agreement, will be enforceable.

X. Language Requirements

Does the law in your country require that a franchise agreement be translated into the local language in order to be enforceable between the parties?

The laws of Nepal do not require that a franchise agreement must be translated into the local language to make it enforceable. For the purpose of approval from DOI, the franchise agreement can either be in Nepalese or English.[32]

XI. Other Significant Matters

Please advise as to whether there are any significant matters not addressed above of which a franchisor should

---

[31] *Contract Act*, §13(a).

[32] *PMFIN*, Pg. 63.

be aware in connection with its entering into a franchise agreement in your country.

There are no franchise associations in Nepal to date. There is no franchised brands specific legislation that has been proposed to be enacted. Some of the notable franchised brands operating in Nepal are - Pizza Hut, KFC, Hyatt, Radisson, Crowne Plaza, etc.

Bibliography of International Franchise Resources

Kendal H. Tyre, Jr., Diana Vilmenay-Hammond, Pierce Haesung Han, Courtney L. Lindsay II and Keri McWilliams
Nixon Peabody LLP
Washington, D.C.

I. General International Resources

Mark Abell, Gary R. Duvall, and Andrea Oricchio Kirsh, *International Franchise Legislation* B1, ABA FORUM ON FRANCHISING (1996)

Kathleen C. Anderson and Anthony M. Stiegler, *Put Muscle in Your Marks: Enforcing Intellectual Property Rights* W14, ABA FORUM ON FRANCHISING (1995)

Richard M. Asbill and Jane W. LaFranchi, *International Franchise Sales Laws—A Survey* W7, ABA FORUM ON FRANCHISING (2005)

Jeffery A. Brimer, Alison C. McElroy, and John Pratt, *Going International: What Additional Restraints Will You Face?* W4, ABA FORUM ON FRANCHISING (2011)

Michael G. Brennan, Alexander Konigsberg, and Philip F. Zeidman, *Globetrotting: A Workshop on International Franchising* 10/W8, ABA FORUM ON FRANCHISING (1994)

Michael G. Brennan, Alexander Konigsberg, and Philip F. Zeidman, *Globetrotting: Strategies for Launching U.S.*

Franchisors Abroad 2/P2, ABA FORUM ON FRANCHISING (1994)

Christopher P. Bussert and Jennifer Dolman, *Regaining Your Trademark After Abandonment or Misappropriation* W7, ABA FORUM ON FRANCHISING (2011)

Ronald T. Coleman and Linda K. Stevens, *Trade Secrets and Confidential Information: Rights and Remedies* W2, ABA FORUM ON FRANCHISING (2000)

Finola Cunningham, *Commerce Department Helps Franchisors Go Global,* in FRANCHISING WORLD 63 (Dec. 2005)

Michael R. Daigle and Alex S. Konigsberg, *Meeting Off-Shore Disclosure and Contract Requirements* F/W13, ABA FORUM ON FRANCHISING (1992)

Jennifer Dolman, Robert A. Lauer, and Lawrence M. Weinberg, Structuring International Master Franchise Relationships for Success and Responding When Things Go Awry W22, ABA FORUM ON FRANCHISING (2007)

Gary R. Duvall, Paul Jones, and Jane LaFranchi, *Planning for the International Enforcement of Franchise Agreements* W6, ABA FORUM ON FRANCHISING (1999)

William Edwards, International Expansion: Do Opportunities Outweigh Challenges? in FRANCHISING WORLD (February 2008)

George J. Eydt and Stuart Hershman, *Bringing a Foreign Franchise System to the United States* W9, ABA FORUM ON FRANCHISING (2009)

William A. Finkelstein and Louis T. Pirkey, *International Trademarks* W15, ABA FORUM ON FRANCHISING (1991)

William A. Finkelstein, Protecting Trademarks Internationally: Current Strategies and Developments B3, ABA FORUM ON FRANCHISING (1996)

Stephen Giles, Lou H. Jones, and Lawrence Weinberg, *Negotiating and Documenting Complex International Franchise Agreements* W21, ABA FORUM ON FRANCHISING (2006)

Steven M. Goldman, Stephen Giles, Marc Israel, and Stanley Wong, *Competition Round Up from Around the World* LB2, ABA FORUM ON FRANCHISING (2004)

David C. Gryce and E. Lynn Perry, *Trademarks and Copyrights in the International Arena* 6/W4, ABA FORUM ON FRANCHISING (1993)

Kenneth S. Kaplan, Andrew P. Loewinger, and Penelope J. Ward, *System Standards in International Franchising* W14, ABA FORUM ON FRANCHISING (2005)

Edward Levitt and Jorge Mondragon, A Survey of International Legal Traps and How to Avoid Them—Beyond the Franchise Laws W20, ABA FORUM ON FRANCHISING (2007)

Ned Levitt, Kendal H. Tyre, and Penny Ward, *The Impossible Dream: Controlling Your International Franchise System* W4, ABA FORUM ON FRANCHISING (2010)

Michael K. Lindsey and Andrew P. Loewinger, *International (Non-U.S.) Franchise Disclosure Requirements* W9, ABA FORUM ON FRANCHISING (2002)

Andrew P. Loewinger and John Pratt, *Recent Changes and Trends in International Franchise Laws* W4, ABA FORUM ON FRANCHISING (2008)

Andrew P. Loewinger and Thomas M. Pitegoff, Avoiding the Long Arm of the Law in International Franchising: Issues and Approaches W8, ABA FORUM ON FRANCHISING (1995)

Craig J. Madson and Katherine C. Spelman, *Similarity and Confusion in the Intellectual Property Arena* W11, ABA FORUM ON FRANCHISING (1997)

Christopher A. Nowak, John Pratt, and Carl E. Zwisler, *Franchising Internationally with Countries with Opaque Legal Systems* W20, ABA FORUM ON FRANCHISING (2006)

E. Lynn Perry and John L. Sullivan Jr., *Trademark Compliance and Enforcement Techniques* E/W12, ABA FORUM ON FRANCHISING (1992)

Marcel Portmann, *Franchising Sector Proves Global Reach*, in FRANCHISING WORLD (January 2007)

John Pratt and Luiz Henrique O. do Amaral, Civil Law for Common Law Practitioners (or How to Draft an Agreement for Use Overseas) W4, ABA FORUM ON FRANCHISING (2002)

Kirk W. Reilly, Robert F. Salkowski and Geoffrey B. Shaw, *Determining the Rules of Engagement in Litigation Here and Abroad* W5, ABA FORUM ON FRANCHISING (2008)

Catherine Riesterer and Frank Zaid, *Basics of International Franchising* L/B2, ABA FORUM ON FRANCHISING (1997)

W. Andrew Scott and Christopher N. Wormald, *Stranger in a Strange Land: Contrasting Franchising in International Expansion* W2, ABA FORUM ON FRANCHISING (2003)

Donald Smith and Erik Wulff, *International Franchising: The Unraveling of an International Franchise Relationship* 15/W13, ABA FORUM ON FRANCHISING (1993)

Frank Zaid, Pamela Mills, and Michael Santa Maria, *Essential Issues in International Franchising* LB/1, ABA FORUM ON FRANCHISING (2001)

II. Asian Resources

Stephen Giles, Andrew P. Loewinger, and Sherin Sakr, *Go East Young Franchisor: Franchising in Asia-Pacific Other Than China and India* W21, ABA FORUM ON FRANCHISING (2011)

Stephen Giles, *Franchising in Asia-Pacific Region, Who's Who Legal*: FRANCHISE 2012 (2012)

A. China

Ren Yanling, *Changes to Chinese Franchise Law: An improved Balance Between the Interests of Franchisors and Franchisees*, in INT'L JOURNAL OF FRANCHISING LAW 3 (2012)

China: New Franchsing Law, in Int'l Journal of FRANCHISING LAW 2 (2005)

Ella S.K. Cheong, *China*, in INTERNATIONAL FRANCHISING CHN/1 (Dennis Campbell gen. ed. 2011)

Yu Qin and Richard L. Wageman, *China*, in INTERNATIONAL FRANCHISE SALES LAWS China-1 (Andrew P. Loewinger and Michael K. Lindsey eds. 2010)

Mark Abell, Daniela C. Brito, and Paul D. Jones, *Franchising in the BRIC Markets (Brazil, Russia, India, and China)* W18, ABA FORUM ON FRANCHISING (2008)

B. Hong Kong

Andrea S.Y. Fong, *Hong Kong*, in INTERNATIONAL FRANCHISING HK/1 (Dennis Campbell gen. ed. 2011)

C. India

Preeti Mehta, *India—Termination of Master Franchise Agreements and the Consequences*, in INT'L JOURNAL OF FRANCHISING LAW 3 (2007)

Yoginder Pal, *Franchising in India*, FRANCHISING WORLD (October 2006)

Mark Abell, Daniela C. Brito and Paul D. Jones, *Franchising in the BRIC Markets (Brazil, Russia, India, and China)* W18, ABA FORUM ON FRANCHISING (2008)

D. Indonesia

Sigit Ardianto and Rivan F. Ramadhan, *Indonesia*, in INTERNATIONAL FRANCHISING INA/1 (Dennis Campbell gen. ed. 2011)

Rick Beckman and Ferry P. Madian, *Indonesia*, in INTERNATIONAL FRANCHISE SALES LAWS Indonesia-1 (Andrew P. Loewinger and Michael K. Lindsey eds. 2010)

Kendal H. Tyre, Jr. & Pierce Haesung Han, *The Ministry of Trade of Indonesia Limits Growth of Food and Beverage*

Franchises, NIXON PEABODY LLP: FRANCHISE ALERT (February 2013)

E. Japan

Takenari Shimizu, *Japan*, in INTERNATIONAL FRANCHISING JAP/1 (Dennis Campbell gen. ed. 2011)

Souichirou Kozuka and Takashi Kanai, *Japan*, in INTERNATIONAL FRANCHISE SALES LAWS Japan-1 (Andrew P. Loewinger and Michael K. Lindsey eds. 2010)

F. Malaysia

Leela Baskaran, *Malaysia*, in INTERNATIONAL FRANCHISING MAY/1 (Dennis Campbell gen. ed. 2011)

Mohd Bustaman Hj Abdullah and Wong Sai Fong, *Malaysia*, in INTERNATIONAL FRANCHISE SALES LAWS Malaysia-1 (Andrew P. Loewinger and Michael K. Lindsey eds. 2010)

Kendal H. Tyre, Jr. & Pierce Haesung Han, *Malaysian Government Actively Promotes Growth in Franchise Sector*, NIXON PEABODY LLP: FRANCHISE ALERT (October 2013)

Kendal H. Tyre, Jr. & Pierce Haesung Han, *Tapping Into Malaysia's Aggressive Franchising Goals*, PORTFOLIO MEDIA, INC.: LAW360 (November 2013)

G. Singapore

Daniel Lim, Bernard Lui, Michele The, and Vanessa Chew, *Singapore*, in INTERNATIONAL FRANCHISING SIN/1 (Dennis Campbell gen. ed. 2011)

H. South Korea

Brendon Carr and Jae-Hoon Kim, *South Korea*, in INTERNATIONAL FRANCHISE SALES LAWS South Korea-1 (Andrew P. Loewinger and Michael K. Lindsey eds. 2010)

I. Taiwan

Wellington Liu and David Lu, *Taiwan*, in INTERNATIONAL FRANCHISE SALES LAWS Taiwan-1 (Andrew P. Loewinger and Michael K. Lindsey eds. 2010)

J. Thailand

Alan Adcock and Sriwan Puapondh, *Thailand*, in INTERNATIONAL FRANCHISING THA/1 (Dennis Campbell gen. ed. 2011)

K. Vietnam

Mai Minh Hang and Nguyen Anh Tran, *Vietnam*, in INTERNATIONAL FRANCHISE SALES LAWS Vietnam-1 (Andrew P. Loewinger and Michael K. Lindsey eds. 2010)

Printed in Dunstable, United Kingdom

91343663R00022